Returning

Poems by
Rich Green

Kokopelli & Lemmy Dog Press
Boulder, Colorado

Life in her myriad colors
returns us home to ourselves.
– Rich Green

"Yolanda's Return" was first published in chapbook, *Poems of the
Great West*, 1989; secondly published in *World of Great Poems*, 1989.

"Simply: Shot in the Neck" was first published in *Skywriting 6*, 1983.

"The Madonna della Pietà," "Remembering Cesar Chavez,"
"Rusting Sun," "Town and Country," and "Desert Walks" were first
published in *earthstone poems by rich green*, 1973.

Title: *Returning*
Author: Rich Green
Cover photographs: Rich Green
    front: Wet Mt. Valley, Westcliffe, CO
    back: Gold Hill, CO
Layout: Ann Erwin
ISBN #979-8-218512-16-3
Published by Kokopelli & Lemmy Dog Press, Boulder, CO

IN MEMORY OF

AUNT RHODA
supporter of the arts

ANNIE SEABECK
my precious wife and best friend:
a person who never stopped believing

ETHEL KENNEDY
RFK Center for Justice and Human Rights
a true role model and advocate
for a "just and peaceful world"

To this day my spiritual life is found
  inside the heart of the wild.
I do not fear it, I court it.
When I am away, I anticipate my return,
  needing to touch stone, rock, water, the trunks
  of trees, the sway of grasses, the barb of a feather,
  the fur left behind by a shedding bison.
      – Terry Tempest Williams
         conservationist, activist, American author and educator

HERE

Here a snail on a wet leaf
shivers and dreams of spring.
Here a green iris in December.
Here the topaz light of the sky.
Here one stops, hearing a twig
break and listens for deer...
      – Arthur Sze
         from The Redshifting Web: Poems 1970–1998
         author of eleven books of poetry

I want to think again of dangerous and noble things.
I want to be light and frolicsome.
I want to be improbable, beautiful, and afraid of
  nothing,
as though I had wings.
      – Mary Oliver (1939–2019)
         American poet and essayist

IN THE MOUNTAIN TENT

I am hearing the shape of the rain
Take the shape of the tent and believe it,
Laying down all around where I lie
A profound, unspeakable law.
I obey, and am free-falling slowly...
      – James Dickey (1923–1997)
        American poet and novelist

When I first read and heard these words above,
I knew at that moment
      I wanted to be a poet!
        – Rich Green

ϙ CONTENTS

Returning

♪ YOLANDA'S RETURN

It's   in the earth   the red soil
It   flows within her veins
It's   within her people   it's all around her

It's   within the sky
It's   within sunlight on clay
It's   within creekbeds (arroyos)
It's   within churches; small altars
It's   within her people   it's all around her

It's   within her soul
It's   within the sunsets
It's   within sunlight on hollyhocks
It's   within her gaze
It's   within her return

It's   in the earth   the red soil
It   flows within her veins
It's   within the sage/the piñon
It's   within the shadow
It's   within the light
It's   within her waking
It's   within her dreaming
It's   within the land   returning her

First published in chapbook, *Poems of the Great West*, 1989

♞ A HORSE'S EYES: A SUNDAY MORNING

When you look
into a horse's eyes,
the Universe is revealed ...
warmth, tenderness, unconditional love.
When you brush her mane,
we brush the hair of all living things:

      gently stroking
      gentle movement
      gently stroking
      gentle movement

sending pulses   throughout
her living, breathing body ...
strengthening our spiritual
foundations in the process.
When a horse shifts her weight
from hoof to hoof,
she tells us about her discomfort
And we must care for her —
to restore her equilibrium
to restore our equilibrium.

When you offer her sweet oats,
it's a sort of peace offering
to the world.
When you drop the brush
to the earth,
      Einstein's theory of relativity —
space, time, matter come into play.

This horse is majestic!
She embraces all of our human differences...
weakness, joy, sorrow, suffering, confusion.
She restores us;
allowing, forgiving, teaching, holding us,
        revealing Grace,
offering us strength and clarity.

Yes!
When you look into a horse's eyes,
she   holds us.

❦ CHILDREN OF BOATS

Run to America   as fast as you can
Run child run   swim to America
Boat to America   get to America
as fast as you can.

Sometimes when I look into your Asian eyes,
I see the reflection of the soft
        blue green skies
Still, on other days, I see the clouds
        blanketing your eyes.
Closer still, before you turn away,
I see so clearly your memories.
Your father   holds you   holds you
under his torn jacket   covering
delicate eyes.
But, because you are just a child,
you peep through the coat's thin lining.

In your tearful eyes
        I see children
                falling
from ships   into the sea
                drowning.

I hear   through your eyes
        hold on   don't drown you cry.
        Take hold   don't fall   don't die!
There is silence in your eyes.

Run to America   as fast as you can
Run child run   swim to America
Boat to America   get to America
as fast as you can.

I don't know how many days or months
it took you, to walk to or run to
your Boat — your vessel of escape.

I don't know how many hours or days
    you   stood motionless ...
muscles   cramped and packed against others
I don't know how many days
      your small stomach hungered.
I don't know how many days or months
      you   were   lost at sea.

I don't know how many countries
      turned you away
turned you around   sent you away
turned you around   sent you away.

But, by the time you reached America
      you   were no longer a child.
Since that time
      seasons like the ocean tides
have come and gone
      come and gone.
And, with the seasons
    emerged your most precious smile.

This poem is based on a true story as shared with me by one of
my Vietnamese students.

❧ SMALL BIRDS

Freedom is a sweet thing
and when the core essence
of it is threatened, we can
      bend   in half
      break   like a twig
or when the foundation is strong,
mountain winds of huge magnitude
can rock this house   and
      it will be sustained.
Anger turned to raw violence...
upheaval — is a clear and present danger
to the integrity of this sweet thing.
We cradle it ... hold it.
We cup it. We drink from these
streams of life   that flow to the sea.
      Vision   is restored.
Loving this concept called freedom —
      protecting it,   is often a delicate balance
as is freedom of expression/speech.

So, with three days until the swearing in,
      troops begin to amass.
Barbed wire stretches   attempting
to protect a ritual.
Force on this day is not in
harmony with normality.

"Love in the time" of COVID is fragile,
      as is freedom.
We take in a collective breath
And hope that sunshine
will embrace us upon this land.
We look forward to Spring

to cherry blossoms   that magnify
our hope   engender sweetness.
Kindness   compassion
        encompass the hearts
        of the newly elected.

This thing   freedom
comes with a price.
Perhaps compromise
        heals a festered wound.
We believe   small birds
with lovely songs will bring harmony.
        It is not written.
        It is only a dream
                and cherished wish.

This poem occurred around the time of Joe Biden's swearing-in
ceremony as the 46th President of the United States and the
questioned Trump insurrection.

ANNIE

(in memory of my precious wife)

In my dream
I tried to keep her near
and safe and warm.
In my dream
her garden thrived,
as she took great and loving care
to tend to the orange poppies, blue iris,
fragrant phlox, pink lupine,
and many more flowers with lovely names.

Day in – day out – she
weeded with tenderness and strength:
her feet planted steadfast
in the earth ... her entire being
immersed in the moment.
In her garden she lost herself —
in great Joy
in great Beauty.

Oh, gardener of life!
Oh, gardener of Life!

The world's woes and concerns
fall to fertile and unencumbered ground.
So too, as in life,
flowers begin to fade,
petals begin to fall.

The garden and gardener
had become one.

In my dream
I tried to keep her safe
and warm and near.

She looked up at me
through flowered labyrinth
And, with a sweet and fragrant smile,
she said —
"I am okay."

SHE RISES

      Gradually
          Gradually
she rises
      illuminating   ablazing
      pine tree tops
      illuminating   ablazing
crystalline   diamonds
      ... our last snowfall.

      Gradually
          Gradually
I rise
      with sunlight
in my heart
      and
diamonds in my eyes.

§ GAZING UPON AN ORANGE POPPY

Looking deeply
into the heart and soul
    of the poppy flower —
other worlds with other dimensions
revealed — breathless designs —
breathless patterns   leave me
transported to where I know not.

This poppy holds me ... transfixed.
It is more than a gaze
that questions all things and floods
my mind with memories.
What color compassion?
What shape forgiveness?
What fragrance a poem?
What subtle hands of cherished flower
rock me sweetly and oh,
so gently?

Tender   tender are her orange petals
gracing   gracing our friendship
cultivated
touching   touching the many travels
we have shared together.

Such complicated growth
    with deep roots
bending
    our spirits towards light
And an evolving Love.

THE MYSTERY OF TREES

What propels them
      to reach   to reach   to reach
      towards blue unfettered sky
30 years ago   mere sticks protruding
      through earthsoil
Now   present tense
      50   60   70 feet tall
Sunlight bathes them
Water feeds them
And then there is spirit
      of community —
roots connecting one another
as they speak a common language:
growth   heal   care   beauty.

It's all right there!
Their leaves soon will drop
to earth carried by Fall-sweet wind.
Their leaves once again will decay
      providing nourishment
for future generations.
And so it goes.
A blessed mystery
      of
Renewal and Hope!

❧ A PIECE OF FRUIT

If only I could offer you
    a piece of fruit,
there would be peace

If only I could offer
your child a piece of fruit,
the swollen belly of hunger
    would disappear

And, as your perilous journey
continues endlessly escaping
violence   oppression   unspeakable crimes
against you, I so wish
I could give you a piece of fruit
    instead of barbed wire

You are the displaced
    seeking a refuge
of lotus flowers and kindness:
an eternal flame of compassion
    and hope
      to place in your woven baskets

Ah — so many scarred refugees-immigrants
    innocent casualties of war
seemily trekking endlessly
    towards a safe haven

If only your villages and cities
    were restored,
your hearts would call forth
"Embrace me. Embrace me.
    For this could be you."

₰ SUCH BEAUTY

How can there be such beauty
    as sunlight
        caresses
    the underside
        of the giant catalpa leaves?

How can there be such beauty
as the impeccable
    sound of stream water   flowing
over rocks   smoothing them
as time has done
    over and over
        for an inordinate length?

And the beauty of the sound
of my feet   against the earth,
as I hike   this trail
    repeatedly
    over and over
        for an inordinate length?

And how about the meteorite
that contains carbon and water
indicative of
    the formation of
planet Earth and her beauty
    to sustain life?

I am overwhelmed with pure Joy
    as the winds of Fall
    speak a tongue
        that I understand.

Beauty around us —
Beauty inside of us —
      as the solar eclipse
      prepares to catch
          our imagination.

We welcome the calm
      the peace
      the complexity
      the simplicity
the sweet nectar
      of it all!

This poem was inspired by a PBS program.

PINE NEEDLES

Lay out your blanket
sweet and soft
Place a Chinese lacquered vase
with cut flowers
in the folds of the center

Place the freshly-baked bread
to the left of the vase
to the right of the wine
And dream love
until the wine bottle bursts

LEANING INTO MY GARDEN
(in memory of Annie & Bev)

I lean into my garden —
    gratitude blossoms.
Delphiniums, columbines, lilies, celosia, coral bells;
    allies that speak truth.
My eyes seek out the architecture
of my home —
curves, lines, brick and wood ...
protection against the elements,
thankful for all of this:
from the sleek blade of grass
to wildflowers encompassing patio.
In a few days friends arrive,
bringing sweetgrass baskets of love
to be planted deep within the soil
of my heart.

I know there are brothers and
sisters in war-ravaged Ukraine
and refugees in all parts of the world.
I take in a deep breath
for all who suffer — breathing out hope
that one day, they too,
can lean into
their freshly-planted gardens.

JAZZ MAN

jazz man   black orchid man
maker of sweet pure sound
resonating and blossoming forth
speaking a soulful language ...
a language we can get lost in ...
a sometimes calm language that connects and reconnects:
     things   spaces   objects   people
to one another.

Sounds created out of pain or gifts of ease
orchestrated within the jazzman's heart
     the very soul of him
where oceanic patterns   carry and reemerge
filter light and beauty
synthesizing note upon note
sending trumpeter's vision   across vast territories
     vast regions
bridging   and once again   connecting the music for us ...

a sweet   pure   sound
   more beautiful
     more unique
       than a black orchid in full bloom.

ENDURING FRIENDSHIP

The catalpa leaves rustle ...
Nancy's lone crow
    caws comfort
        in
            distant tree.

❧ BECKY AND THE MOTHERS OF LEBANON: A SLEEPLESS NIGHT

She sleeps black of raven's hair
    across my pillow.
She breathes air into air and out again
She breathes air into air and out again
I suck in her air into my air and out again.

The raven screeches overhead.

Two bodies intertwined like twigs or sticks igniting.
I am silent.

Visions soar in the dark deep of night.
Women mothers of children caught in the crossfire
        hundreds of them
    screeching, screaming; sirening out
        from the contracted muscle
           of throat and heart...
Allah, Allah, my babies are dying!
Strained-dried eyes no longer capable of tears.
Strained-dried voices no longer capable of words.

She sleeps black of raven's hair
    across my pillow.
She breathes air into air and out again.
Her fingers curled around my fingers
    like tree roots curled around exposed rocks.
She murmurs out cries or utterances.

The raven circles, overhead.

I soft-kiss her forehead.
More visions soar in the dark deep of night.

Beirut is burning   igniting!
Moments before young boy soldiers
        ambulatory in the aimless, machine-gun spray ...
        now motionless on green canvas stretchers
        as Beirut burns fire into the sides
        of once living-breathing-dreaming youth.

She is still.

She sleeps black of raven's hair
        across my pillow.
The dark deep of night
        unfolds her grip on light.

I ask her if she would like tea before she leaves.
She says, No, thank you.
        kisses my lips with tenderness
        and says, You look exhausted.

On June 6, 1982, Israeli forces launched a three-pronged invasion
of southern Lebanon in "Operation Peace for Galilee."

❦ SANGRE DE CRISTOS

She   steals me away
as sunlight breaks
        over the Sangres
        revealing red
as shadows lift   over
        lush green meadows   green pastures
            all interspersed with wild blue iris
        and herds of cattle with heads bowed
        downward towards the green and
                luscious earth

She steals me away
with her logged houses   expansive barns
quiet cemeteries   centuries-old homesteads
        as a calm and silent
wind blows here in the Wet Mountain Valley,
        as it always has

And her spirit once was
        the rush for silver:
dreams carried within covered wagons
while footwalkers traversed
the land from faraway places
        leaving behind the known
for the unknown

Disease took some of them
        on this treacherous journey West
        — small white crosses
            reminders of their sacrifices

And yet, they came to Colorado
to settle towns
    Rosita   Querida
    Silver Cliff   Westcliffe
all with the promise of a rich future
for these beleaguered   yet
    hopeful settlers
seeking large parcels of land
    for their families and beloved horses
against the backdrop of the
    Sangre de Cristos

Ah, she steals my heart away
    with solid memories of the past
as the exquisite Beauty
      of the present
   offers herself
      introduces me
      to a new kind of place

℔ THE WHITE HYACINTH

The rain dances within   the melody
of infinite proportions   grand variations
in this atmospheric collision of droplets.
First a soft sound
then a pounding heavier sound
then a return to a soft note
then a return to a pounding heavier note
        in this balanced orchestra of Nature.

Just as the newly growing
            newly forming
        white hyacinth
dances on the cool surface of rain
        on this cool eve
rhythm exists in a shared movement
        with Nature.
The rain begs us to listen —
        then returns us — soft droplets.
All is quiet ...
        Simple beauty   simple harmony.

The solitary white hyacinth
shimmers light
        in the deep
wet darkness of night.

THE VIRUS

Guide me through this maze,
direct my footsteps towards peace,
free me of fear.
Let us embrace one another.
Let us grieve for the losses
and hold one another tightly.
Help me to see things differently —
to develop a new perspective:
to see life as sacred.
To realize I honestly don't have the
answers; however, I am steadfast
in my pursuit.
These times of critical virus will pass.
Life will resume to a new normal
and give hope to our renewed dreams,
renewed beliefs, and new focus.
Learning is hard; overcoming adversity
is much harder.
Strengthen our cores and help mold
us into more compassionate beings.
Through this intense crisis, give us
our breath back, our compass
purposeful, our lives differently
better; our capacity for love enlarged.

DAUGHTERS OF GENTLE BEINGS
for Laurel and Nancy

Yes! You both are daughters
        of gentle parents
weaned on kindness
        transmitted
flowing through your veins
to the Beauty of your hair and eyes.
Your mother   special gardener
of splendid cosmos and myriad
humble flowers ... she remembers
turning soil, as her parents once did.

Yes! You sing the praises
        of your ancestral connection —
respecting their connection
        to earth   mountains   plains...
all kind and brave homesteaders.
And as time passed, the two of you
evolved and continue to evolve
into gentle beings
as you walk in harmony
        upon this earth.

♬ GLORY

I take
I take
I take
    in
        the captivating sunset
        over my Flatirons.

I am mesmerized
    mesmerized
        mesmerized
until words drop from my tongue
pouring into a pool
        of red.

I try to walk
    the distance
between sunset and home
transfixed I am
consumed with the
    glory
        of it all!

♬ BEV'S DANCE

Life gave birth to Bev
and the earth began to sing
and jazz resonated in her heart ...
in our hearts. And the message was love!

I remember hearing of this young beauty
in Trieste, Italy; her formative year
when her journey began. What did you see?
What songs touched your heart? Did you know
about Berlin and beyond borders?
How did you know that you would embrace us
and slip gingerly into our hearts
and envelope us with your
unconditional love?

Years passed   seasons came.
Your tender hands and
your sweet laughter began
to help others: nursing them
to renewed health; a life-long
purpose of an opened heart,
a joyful spirit, a kind soul.

And then you gave birth
to two creative souls.
And the earth celebrated.
And there were immense tears
of joy.
Jazz was born,
theater was enriched.

You were there throughout our lives.
You were there to dance us
through hard times
And gentle times.
Your light empowered us.
And for this we are forever touched
by your grand Beauty — grand Love.

And in the past several days, bird feathers
have appeared throughout my yard,
whispering the message:
"Take flight, dear Bev, take flight!"

A POEM TO CALM THE 1986 PERSON
or
A BEDTIME POEM FOR CHILDREN

sweet falling softly
white on white
settled silence

sweet, sweet falling
     listless
and ever downward
white on white
settled silence

Fall softly oh my sweet
white gown on night
and ever downward

Hush — she whispers
oh my love
sweet so sweet
     white on white
settled silence
     sweet falling softly ...
          Hush.

ᚦ THIS FIRE IS PRAYER

This fire is prayer.

It is snowing   continually
      continually
            continually.
Waves of whiteness
     in this direction
     in that direction
soft floating
     onto earthen ground
— snuggles on boughs
     of evergreens   junipers.
There is no name for snow.
Each snowflake unique
in shape   in content
waiting for the deep dive ...
elicits: joy   fear   contentment

But the winter garden,
     it knows —
opens her arms
     to this blessing
     to this blessing.

♪ THE SORROW OF THE SAXOPHONE
(in memory of Michael Clifton, great Berlin jazz
drummer and my younger brother)

I didn't know
    didn't comprehend
    the true meaning of jazz
    the journey into a cacophony
        of sound.
But if I listen   feel   open
    my heart   my soul
    much much is to be revealed.
Just ask jazz saxophonist Joshua Redman
as he shares deep deep
    powerful   messages   insights
    with me   opening   a musical
    landscape to me
        as two diverse musical pieces
    reside side by side —
        an artistry   creativity
    into my realm of comprehension.

I didn't know
    didn't comprehend
    the transformative indelible palate
    of patterns   notes   sounds
        a working composition —
    Redman gifted me.

"Alabama" by John Coltrane
    and "After Minneapolis (face toward
    mo[u]rning)" by Joshua Redman
        interpret oh-so-sadly
    two historical black events.
"Alabama" embraces death —
    four African-American girls
        murdered inside 16th Street
        Baptist Church by the Ku Klux Klan

here on Sept 15, 1963
And Coltrane's saxophone
        cries out in utter grief
                utter pain
questions   questions this horrific
scene   Why?   Why? did this
racial injustice happen here in Amerika?
The saxophone accentuates the horror,
the anguish in dissonant notes
crying forth this senseless act —
        leaving me breaking.

And then, a shift to
"After Minneapolis (face toward mo[u]rning)"
Redman's sax in dissonant notes
dissonant sounds reveals another composition
— too difficult to hold!

Yes, May 25, 2020, a black man
George Floyd is murdered
by a white cop ... another —
innocent lost.
There is no rhyme or meter
for these deaths.
There is no juxtaposition between
        these two jazz pieces.
I never knew   never comprehended
until now
        stories told   stories
revealed by the sorrow
of the saxophone.
If the blue note exists,
        this must be it.

This poem was inspired by a PBS program.

₵ WRITER'S TRUTH

Bring me towards silence
so I may hear ...
silent breath in winter calm.
white snow-covered milkweed
        invites me inward.
Teach me gratitude
in my walk upon the earth:
to look upon woods   frozen creeks
wind-swept meadows.
Keep my heart alert for coyotes
hawks   ravens   kingfishers   prairie dogs ...
and the unexpected.

Teach me the Four Directions,
        so I may find my way.
Impart understanding
        of the connectedness of all things.

Let me embrace the gifts of the Earth
and, in return, give something back.
Above all else,
        let compassion guide me.

Inspired by *Braiding Sweetgrass* by Robin Wall Kimmerer, 2013.

THE WONDER OF IT ALL

They squeak.
They squeal.
They scream ...
  I guess that's what children do.

And the leaves
  twist and turn
  titter and toss
As western winds
  release
   their hold.

And, yes!
   Gravity
 does
 the
rest.

♀ A SONG FOR THE EARTH

To smell the earth
is to love
that which is grand,
that which is small.
To see the leaf embedded
in the snow
is to know
the richness of the land.
To understand the seasons
that cycle through life,
death and renewal,
is to connect   with the divine,
                   with the infinite.
To appreciate the eclipses of
moon and sun
is to be rich in imagination.
To feel the beauty
of love and friendship
on a cold winter's night
is a treasured gift.

To be grateful
for loss, although it hurts;
it, too, holds a vastness ...
a wealth of cherished memories.

To know we can turn to the desert
for comprehension of the struggle
for meaningful survival.

To witness grace and strength
as a father and mother hold
their children
during ice and fire.

To comprehend history
and the politics of the mind
gives hope when darkness descends.

And, with all of our walks and hikes,
we step into gratitude
with the memory
of the smell of the land.

⚕ YANKEE

to Daniel, my nephew, who encouraged me to talk
about the Vietnam War

I awakened this morning to a very vivid memory of
    the past.
"Doc, could you give me my medicine?"
"Doc, could you adjust my sling?"
"Doc, where ya from?"

As I walked down the hospital ward, the injured
Marines and Navy servicemen reached for
human contact: a smile, a handshake, words of
encouragement. As I walked without staring, I
noticed a lot of amputees and a lot of young men in
wheelchairs.

   As my supervisor (nurse and instructor) and
I toured the ward, we approached an emaciated
youth in a circular bed. This large metal apparatus
surrounding him made him appear even smaller than
he actually was. "This is Yankee, your patient for the
next sixteen weeks," the nurse introduced us to one
another.

   Yankee's eyes revealed it all! He was the
embodiment of the Vietnam War: bewilderment
waste   deep sadness   *Great losses without meaning.*
I remember he struggled to shake my hand. Yet his
determination brought his hand forward to grasp
mine. His warm smile eased my fear. We were both 19
years old.

Over the next sixteen weeks, I would care for
Yankee, six to eight hours a day. He was my only
patient. There was much to do each day ... change his
colostomy bag regularly ... replace IVs ... drain open

wounds ... change bandages ... rotate Yankee in the circular bed to prevent decubitus ulcers. And lastly, gently rub lotion onto Yankee's dry and frail body. I don't recall what we talked about during those days. I don't recall where Yankee was from. I don't remember how he became so severely injured. An explosion or multiple gunshots? But I do remember his daily struggle and his demeanor: a quiet confidence guided him.

After sixteen weeks, I left Yankee's side. I left behind the hospital ward at Great Lakes Naval Hospital. I was assigned duty onboard the USS Forrestal, CVA-59, an aircraft carrier. My ship was in drydock being repaired in Norfolk, Virginia, after a disaster in the Tonkin Gulf, Vietnam. I was now a U.S. Navy Hospital Corpsman, a medic.

I don't know to this day what became of Yankee. I don't know if he partially or fully recovered. I don't recall if he had a spinal cord injury that left him paralyzed and incapable of walking. I am not aware of the emotional costs of the war that impacted Yankee's life and whether or not he overcame this trauma as well.

But I do know he taught me humility. Yankee honored me by letting me care for him.

⚘ BROTHERS

Part 1

Once we stood the two of us on a spiritual hill surrounded by petroglyphs in New Mexico ...

On another day in another year we walked along a riverbed of worn rock where a small white cross stood embedded in the earth ... again in New Mexico.

Once we hiked to the top of a large outcropping overlooking Evergreen. The next day you left for Aspen ...

Always, there was wind blowing on each of these days, reminding us of what was to come. Do you remember what the wind spoke?

Part 2   THE WIND SPOKE

Be still oh restless searcher of Truth
    Quiet thy mind and accept what life offers
The Truth surrounds you
    Be attentive and experience it in all of its
Creation
It is not a mystery
    It is Truth
           – Peter Green, aka Pedro de Cedro

As we stood on a hill below the Sierra Blanca, surrounded by spirits of the past, this is what the wind spoke. – Pedro de Cedro

⸎ SIMPLY: SHOT IN THE NECK

There is no rhyme or meter for death.
Death seems inappropriate
when you're shot in the neck.
The jugular vein that sustains life
is our worst enemy
when severed by a raw bullet.
There is nothing fair about a wife's bloodcurdling scream
that wakes everyone including the giant cottonwood
in the extreme hours of the morning.
There is nothing fair about the Chicano boy who
experienced the scream
the reverberation of the bullet
the blood-soaked carpet.
There is no rhyme or meter for death.
Death seems inappropriate
when you're shot in the neck.
And when I asked the boy what happened
he said, matter of factly,
"Chester got blown away last night.
He got shot in the neck."

❧ I CLOSE MY EYES

I close my eyes
I hear the water
lapping over the heavenly roots
of apple tree, lilac bush, rose of Sharon.
I am not a gardener of Life
like some I know, but strive to hike
the trails and backwoods;
as my tendons, ligaments, muscles
crunch the unstable rocks below.
I search out the songmakers and the glorious:
Towhee, Lazuli bunting, Yellow-breasted chat,
Bullock's oriole.
Few I have seen, but accept that fact.

I am surrounded by rocks:
grand elephants slanting red towards
clear and unfettered sky.
This is my destiny.
Hiking Towhee Trail merging at South Mesa,
then Shadow Canyon. I choose Shadow Canyon;
something I've been doing for years.
Sweat trickles like shards of flint.
Fields of beebalm make their calling.

I press on. I move much slower now,
but press on, knowing that Beauty
awaits me.
My body says stop — my heart, yes!
I hear the sound of water — sweet trickle
does it no justice, amidst a country
torn at the shirtsleeves. Once I stared
at bear scat on this earthen path, fearing
the bear's presence.

I turned into a near
miss — a huge snake rattling away,
giving me a heartsharp awakening ...
knowing that if the bear doesn't get me,
something else might.

I turn into a slight wind ... relief from
the heatball of late July.
My faithful internal clock says turn
and return. I resist; however, the rocks,
the earth, the sky, the trees, the wildflowers
say it is alright   to let go.

❦ GREEN TEA

I drink green tea...
this eases the pain
        found within my deepest.
I drink in the eagle chicks
waiting to fledge
high in their nest   their home.
I drink in the capacity
for love found within friends,
family and strangers.
I drink green tea
to celebrate   to honor   to grieve
to resonate
        all who live and those who died.
I drink this tea to illuminate light
and gifted peace.
I drink within   to witness
that which lies below   the surface.

I drink in the poetry
of our dance of Life.
I drink this tea
to harness the demons
wedged within the deepest.

I drink in sorrow and grief
        health and growth.
I drink green tea to connect
with Joshua Bell's "Romance of the Violin."

I drink within to see and feel
the workings of the soul of the earth,
And, for all of this,
I am grateful.

ZAITSEVE

In a small village   eastern Ukraine
two backpacks filled with yesterday's dreams
        reside red
against white crystalline snow.
Village bystanders   in disbelief
        in tearful community sorrow
know in their bones   hearts
that this is just the beginning
of something larger.
In D.C., politicians say "incursion,"
others "invasion." Some say a "small war,"
others, beyond a doubt, say a "full-scale war."
These two soldiers obligated in their patriotism —
now innocence lost.
No such thing as a small war.
Young life lost to an uncertain Ukraine future.
        Throughout the world
                many cry for Zaitseve —
red stains   soft snow.
A village of the once hopeful, now
shiver in the winds of time.
They will remember their two soldiers.

William Faulkner wrote a short story entitled "Two Soldiers."

℥ THE MADONNA DELLA PIETÀ

Before the day,
when the white-marble sun
peers through the willows swaying,
touching the crowned block,
a young man arises from the morning shadows
and walks the dawn rays to his *pietra serena*,
  the quiet stone.

With the clatter of wooden wheels on cobblestone,
oxen lug carts to market
leaving behind the morning solitude.
Drowsy girls gather on the Tiber banks
pounding and scrubbing with rocks their muslin garments
while children sweep the floors of the city
and husky sun-browned women grind yeast
and early cripples beg.

The youth eyes his work,
walks silently around,
soft-touches the tender marble.
  He strikes the slab, hammering shattering crystals,
the stone chips falling across his pained arms,
gray dust rising, matting, clotting his hair and eyes.

He chisels the morning away,
thrusting the quiet stone awake,
  sweeping up the night.

Dropping to the floor,
he dreams in exhausted sleep:
the Virgin lies waiting deep within the stone.
Resuming, he tools, rough-carving,
viciously tearing through the calendar.

His firewood dwindles in the rain mist;
damp cold blankets his shoulders.   He turns,
chilled with god power,
striking downward into the stone.

When the robed thong-footed intruder approaches,
he scowls, steps aside his work, questions,
searches the lines of the old bearded face.
He doesn't smile when the old man nods.
He circles, hammers, hammers.
The old man leaves.

Olive buds open.

After the violent dust has settled,
two forms arise in daylight marble.

To Mary's heart fell child and man.
She holds her pierced son
        close to her.
Michelangelo Buonarroti
    rests his head
        weeps
on the marble shoulder of the Virgin,
        sleeps.

This poem was inspired by reading Irving Stone's *The Agony and the Ecstasy*, 1961.
The *Madonna della Pietà* was completed between 1498–1499.

ꝗ REMEMBERING CESAR CHAVEZ

in the scorching fields   sweat dries
       before it drips
they sit together
resting under the shade of mr raymond's tractor
suncircled eyes   closing
   only for a moment
      then opening
gazing downward
   at the unpicked lettuce

⚡ THE RUSTING SUN

Melinda walks the dust-ringed gaze
        of her eyes
and the dry choking wind
sears the café   where morning-browned
coffee brews for the few lingering

on in this pitted stained town
the bruised working hand   the decayed
        backbone of the rusting sun
the uneasy stir
    of abandoned dogs and lost oilmen
    where stretches of fallen oil dikes
        overturned railroad cars
            and sod houses
await their resurrection   along the
scorched creek   drained   by the insatiable
thirst of the dying
            here
where Melinda walks barefooted across the
    dust-ringed gaze of her eyes
        strutting past the wooden stares
    of men   as earth sweat meanders
                down her bosom
    swaying   in the   orange desert

the one flowering arm of a cactus
                reaches out
to touch her black woven hair
    and the skulls   of the herds
        beckon her

THE PHOTOGRAPHS

I
      haunted
by the image:
           a Palestinian
                child
      standing amidst
      the rubble
           eyes glazed
           in complete
                loss   confusion
      parents missing
           amidst
                devastation.

stark memory
           of a photo —
           a Japanese
                child
      in Hiroshima
      standing amidst
      the rubble
           eyes glazed
           in complete
                loss   confusion
      parents missing
           amidst
                devastation.

The innocent always lose.
No one
      wins
           in
                war.

✀ TOWN AND COUNTRY

I. Town

  the new england sun a veiled candle
    nestles this stilled harbor town
  rising above the calm soft cove
      touching the cove
  through the rain mist
      touching quietly
  the water of the cove
  holding the child of water
      near gibson's sound

II. Country

  to this wooden fence returns
  a man to till the fresh dark loam
  sowing seeds as warblers muse
    rolling forth the stones
  spading uprooting the fallen crops
  where earth and hand meet
      in thompson's field

❦ FIRE AND ICE

Is there time for
    fire and ice?
And, is there room   to hold
    all the sorrow?

preventing a fracture
    of immeasurable magnitude?

Within the ashen soil
    so many memories
    so many times entering   leaving
      leaving and entering.
So many doors gone now —
but, the heart remembers
before fire and ice
    the crashing blow of wind.

Some walk and talk —
    "We will rebuild!" resonates
from this, their wounded tongue.
Others — just seek small things
small items for bare necessity
    carrying on   carrying on.
Earth knows
how long a broken heart
    to mend.

They pass the chalice.
      Together they drink from it...
as so many others
     before them
performed this ritual of healing.
Blue sky melts ashen snow
     holding the chalice ...
        a Promise
             of
                 the Future.

This poem is based on the Marshall Fire in Colorado on
December 30, 2021. In total, 1084 homes were destroyed on this
day. Today – in 2024 – most resilient residents are rebuilding.

♜ WALKING BOB

He's ready.
He's always ready.
Gym bag. Nike running shoes. Nike hat.

Walking Bob walks on.
He's in the groove.
With pride he walks.
With pride he turns.
He could be in a 10K race.
He could be on the beach.
He could be walking at the mall.

He walks with purpose —
strides past Mrs. Kelly of the Bronx
strides past Mrs. Stedman of New Jersey
strides past graying, slumped-over
       figures in wheelchairs.
Been walking for years.
Must stay fit!
Must keep walking.
Walking past Haitian nurses' aides.

However,
       can't remember why I'm here
and not on the beach   the mall
the 10K race.
All I know to be true ...
       is that I'm ready.
I am walking, Bob.
I must walk   must stay fit.

"Remembering sometimes
is not as important as walking, anyway."

Bob was a patient in a memory care unit in Fort Lauderdale, Florida.

៛ DESERT WALKS

she   the lovely Cassandra
         with moonglow breasts
      comforted my desert walks
      moistened my lips   with cactus milk
we   explored the untouched whirling sands
i   burned   with sunfever
       Cassandra's golden body
         shaded mine
      lost in delightful delirium
i   tossed my burntedged calendar
        to the north
      tranquilized by the day's intense heat
she   writhed in motion with the winds
we   counted the sand granules between our toes

₹ HÓZHǪ

Suffer my children   no more
Suffer my children   no more

Like milkweed bursting open
in the Fall of our lives,
my heart, too, cries out
and bursts forth the saddest of tears.

Brothers and sisters of Lebanon Israel
Gaza Syria Ukraine Sudan
The cradle is full: destruction
devastation   unimaginable loss

Our garden withers.
Children of war   lives scarcely begun
           your innocence lost

And, the displaced
    in perpetual movement
questing safe havens
          to rest   shattered lives

As humankind we insist enough
          is enough!

The glimmer of light
on shattered glass
reveals an opening
to harness and engender
          Hope and Peace

Let the disquieted become quiet
and still — to gather
our global response   global strength
            as   one   powerful voice

Netanyahu   violator of your sacred
Hebrew name   "Yah/God has given"
destroyer of sacred life
violator of international human rights law
war criminal of The Hague
not too late   to accept Peace

With seasonal emergence
let gardens   trees   greenness
     return and flourish
where children are nurtured —
            sustained by the beauty of Life.

Suffer my children   no more
Suffer my children   no more

The Navajo word *hózhǫ́* is a complex concept that can be
translated as "peace, balance, beauty, and harmony." It is
considered to be one of the most important words in the Navajo
People's language (*Diné bizaad*).

ꝫ TIME AND TRANSITION

The broken pane of glass
        what remained,
clung   to weathered frame.
There was something strange
        about pierced window.
Shattered fragments of crystal
        glistened slightly
while gray and dim
light cast shadows upon
weed-covered cabin.
Thistle pushed upward
    towards broken glass —
choking last breath of air;
while sage emerged
        everywhere
upon dried soil:
voices from a century past
        remained unheard.
Westerly winds gathered —
    the last piece of hanging glass
        fell
            broke
    into shattered calm.
All that remained or will remain
        is Time.

❦ ACKNOWLEDGMENTS

To the keepers of my poetry: Joan Thale and Nancy George Nichols.

To my poetry mentors: Harry Oliver, Vance Aandal, and James Dickey.

To the youth who continually inspire me: Nyla, Jessica, Aaron, Noah, Benjamin, Foster, Melanie, Chelsey, Kayla, and Queen Esther.

To all the dogs and their owners on Bobolink Trail and Bear Creek Trail.

To all my practitioners in Boulder who keep me walking and hiking, upright and steady. Special gratitude to Ana do Valle and Cathy Koger.

To Christine Summerfield, children's author; Ann Erwin, typesetter; and Linda Liane, author, photographer, and artist, who have guided me towards publication.

To all of my former refugee students from Vietnam, Laos, Cambodia, Somalia, and Afghanistan, who taught me about resilience and compassion; and to the United Nations High Commissioner for Refugees and member Ambassadors for their relentless work for peace throughout the world.

To the Native Americans of Peshawbestown, MI, and Ignacio, CO, who have shared their stories and culture with me; to the American Indian College Fund, Denver, CO, and St. Bonaventure Indian Mission & School, Thoreau, NM, for their meaningful dedication to Native American students and community members.

To my family, friends, and neighbors, who are a huge network of love and support. Special thanks to Kyoko, Nyla, and Petger. Also to Chris and Tsugumi (Ami) Walton, who keep my sails trimmed and my destination clear. I am honored to be Ami's "American Father."

Special thanks to LePeep – Gary, Tori, and Gi – for providing me a space to write.

RICH GREEN is a native of Colorado and long-time resident of Boulder. His work history is varied: tutor and community organizer with Native Americans in VISTA (domestic Peace Corps), ESL teacher/job developer with refugees, Navy Hospital Corpsman, freelance writer, guidance counselor and instructor at Auraria (CO) colleges, photographer, and peace advocate.

The author asserts that writing poetry is a lot like storytelling: Some poems are based upon fact while others are framed solely within the imagination. The themes of RETURNING focus on simple everyday living — listening to ravens, making a cup of green tea, reflecting on the beauty of nature, hiking, exploring ghost towns — while conversely many of the poems ponder the loss of a love, racial injustice, and the profound and devastating effects war has on individual lives: "... no one wins in war."

In RETURNING, Rich's long journey brings him home to himself.

OTHER LITERARY WORKS BY THE AUTHOR

"A Teacher Remembered," essay, *The Monitor*, 1968

"Listen," poem, *Creative Writing Magazine*,
Metropolitan State College of Denver, 1971

Essays about nature and hiking trails, *Evergreen Today*,
1982

"Ghost Town Touring, Colorado," *Camping Life*
magazine, 2003. The author's photographs of Gold
Hill first appeared in this publication.

IN THIS COLLECTION

"Yolanda's Return," chapbook, *Poems of the Great
West* (Certificate of Merit), and *World of Great Poems*
(Golden Poet Award), 1989.

"Simply: Shot in the Neck," *Skywriting 6*; critiqued by
poet and author, James Dickey, 1983.

"The Madonna della Pietà," originally titled "Pieta,
earthstone poems by rich green, 1973.

"Remembering Cesar Chavez," "Rusting Sun," "Town
and Country," and "Desert Walks," *earthstone poems by
rich green*, 1973.

℥ IN PRAISE OF THE POET
and HIS POETRY

Rich's poetry brings me comfort, warmth, joy, and perspective. His words are a gift to all who read them. Their wisdom spreads from Nature to the challenges we all face... Rich, the poet who writes with his heart and follows his own trail.

    – Nancy George Nichols
       author of Memories of Homesteading in the Mountains
       and on the Prairie, *educator, and political activist*

I am blessed to have had Rich Green in my life for over sixty years. He has been my friend, my brother, and a mentor. Having chosen a path in the arts myself, I feel I have some sense of the discipline, passion, and innate talent it takes to "create." Rich has been "creating" from the moment I met him, and his poetry fills me with wonder, joy, awe, and sometimes sadness. I'm sure this publication will do the same for all who have the good fortune to read it.

    – Pam Clifton
       theatre director, actress, writer, and teacher

Rich Green, the gentle poet, has found through the healing arts of poetry, photography, and sketching, the components to strengthen his life and soul. I know you will enjoy his work that I personally name "insights of an autobiography."

    – Ana do Valle
       occupational therapist, life-coach, trauma specialist,
       and Buddhist teacher

www.ingramcontent.com/pod-product-compliance
Lightning Source LLC
Chambersburg PA
CBHW051332120626
46547CB00016B/2510